acoustic love

Published by
Wise Publications
8/9 Frith Street, London, W1D 3JB, England.

Exclusive distributors:

Music Sales Limited
Distribution Centre, Newmarket Road,
Bury St Edmunds, Suffolk, IP33 3YB, England.

Music Sales Pty Limited
120 Rothschild Avenue, Rosebery, NSW 2018, Australia.

Order No. AM984544
ISBN: 1-84609-319-8
This book © Copyright 2006 Wise Publications,
a division of Music Sales Limited.

Cover courtesy of Mental Block Design.
Music processed by Paul Ewers Music Design.

Printed in the United Kingdom.

Your Guarantee of Quality:

As publishers, we strive to produce every book
to the highest commercial standards.

The book has been carefully designed to minimise
awkward page turns and to make playing from it
a real pleasure. Particular care has been given to
specifying acid-free, neutral-sized paper made from pulps
which have not been elemental chlorine bleached.

This pulp is from farmed sustainable forests and
was produced with special regard for the environment.

Throughout, the printing and binding have been planned
to ensure a sturdy, attractive publication which should give
years of enjoyment.

If your copy fails to meet our high standards, please inform us
and we will gladly replace it.

www.musicsales.com

Wise Publications
part of The Music Sales Group
London / New York / Paris / Sydney / Copenhagen / Berlin / Madrid / Tokyo

You're Beautiful

Words & Music by Sacha Skarbek, James Blunt & Amanda Ghost

My life is bril - liant.

won't lose no sleep all night,___ 'cos I've___ got a plan.___

1, 2. You're beau - ti - ful.___   You're beau - ti - ful.___
3. You're beau - ti - ful.___   You're beau - ti - ful.___

You're beau - ti - ful,___ it's true.___   I saw___
You're beau - ti - ful,___ it's true.___   There must___

___ your face   in a   crowd - ed___ place,___
___ be an an - gel   with a   smile on her face___

and I don't know what to do, 'cos I'll nev-
when she

- er be with you.

Yes, she caught

my eye as I walked on by. She could

Sail Away

Words & Music by David Gray

Sail a - way— with me, ho - ney, I put my heart— in your hands.

Sail a - way— with me ho - ney now,— now,— now.—

Sail a - way— with me;— what will be— will be.—

I wan-na hold you— now,—— now,—— now.—

1. Cra - zy skies— all wild— a - bove— me now,

win - ter howl - ing at my face;——

and ev-'ry-thing___ I held___ so dear___

dis-ap-peared___ with-out a trace.___

2. Though all the times___ I tast-ed love,___
(Verse 3 see block lyric)

nev-er knew___ quite___ what I had.

12

Lit - tle dar - ling, if you hear me now,

nev - er need-ed you so bad;

spin-ning 'round in - side my head.

Sail a - way with me, ho - ney, I put my heart in your hands.

Verse 3:
I've been talking drunken gibberish
Falling in and out of bars
Trying to get some explanation here
For the way some people are.
How did it ever come so far?

Chorus 5:
Sail away with me, honey
I put my heart in your hands.
It breaks me up if you pull me down, woh.
Sail away with me; what will be will be.
I wanna hold you now, now, now.

Chorus 6 & 7:
(Whistle)

She Will Be Loved

Words & Music by Adam Levine, James Valentine,
Jesse Carmichael, Mickey Madden & Ryan Dusick

1.

Cm[11]   A[b]add9

be loved._____

2, 3.

A[b]add9 (3° B[b]sus4)   E[b]sus2   B[b]sus4

_____ And she will_____ be loved,_____ and she will__

Cm[11]   A[b]add9   *To Coda* ⊕ Cm

be loved._____ I know where you hide__

B[b]   Cm7   B[b]

a - lone in your car,____ know all of the things__ that make you who you are.____

I know that good-bye____ means no-thing at all,____ comes back and begs me, catch
her ev-'ry time____ she falls._____ Yeah._____
Tap on my win-dow, knock____ on my____ door I
want to make you feel beau-ti-ful._____

D.S. al Coda

Always A Use

Words & Music by Madeleine Peyroux

Emily

Words & Music by Stephen Fretwell

next time you write,___ I won't stay up___ all___ night.. 'Cos E - mi - ly, you,___ well

just look at you:___ you're a tra - ge - dy!

To Coda

D.S. al Coda

Coda

3. You

You

nev-er were gon-na change_ your mind,_ were you,_ an-y - way?_ You

A Smile That Explodes

Words & Music by Joseph Arthur

Original Key D♭ Major

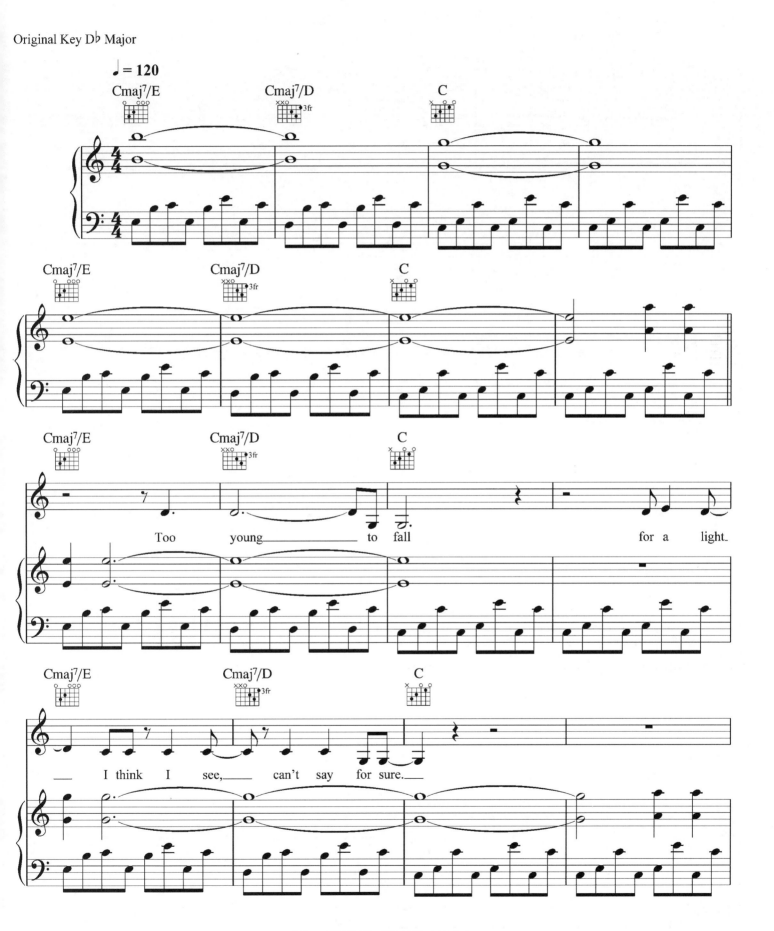

Love And Affection

Words & Music by Joan Armatrading

the friends that I____ want (Lov - er ooh hoo.)

I may need more,__ but I shall just stick to those

that I have got. (Lov - er ooh hoo.)

With friends I still feel so in - se - cure._____

Saxophone

Make love,— oh,———
(Lov - er ooh hoo.)

Wild Wood

Words & Music by Paul Weller

Verse 2:
Don't let them get you down,
Making you feel guilty about
Golden rain will bring you riches,
All the good things you deserve now.

Verse 3:
Climbing, forever trying,
Find your way out of the wild wild wood.
Now there's no justice,
You've only yourself that you can trust in.

Verse 4:
And I said high tide, mid-afternoon,
People fly by in the traffic's boom.
Knowing just where you're blowing,
Getting to where you should be going.

Verse 5:
Day by day your world fades away,
Waiting to feel all the dreams that say,
Golden rain will bring you riches,
All the good things you deserve now.

Ordinary People

Words & Music by Will Adams & John Stephens

Kiss Me

Words & Music by Matt Slocum

1. Kiss me out of the bearded barley. Nightly, beside the green, green grass. Swing, swing, swing the spinning step.

2. Kiss me down by the broken treehouse. Swing me upon it's hanging door. Bring, bring, bring your flowered hat.

You wear those shoes and I will_____ wear that dress.
We'll take the trail marked on your_____ fa-ther's map.

Oh,_____

Kiss___ me_____ be-neath the milk - y twi - light.

Lead___ me_____ out on the moon - lit floor._____

___ Lift your op - en hand,_ strike up the band_ and make_ the

fire-flies dance,_ sil-ver moon's spark - ling._ So kiss

1.

me.

2.

me. La, la, la,___ la, la, la,_

_ la, la, la.___ La, la, la, la,_

la, la, la,_____ la, la, la._____

Ah,

D.S. al Coda

Coda

me.

Someone Else's Song

Words & Music by Jeff Tweedy

1. I can't tell you a-ny-thing,
2. You already know the sto-ry,___

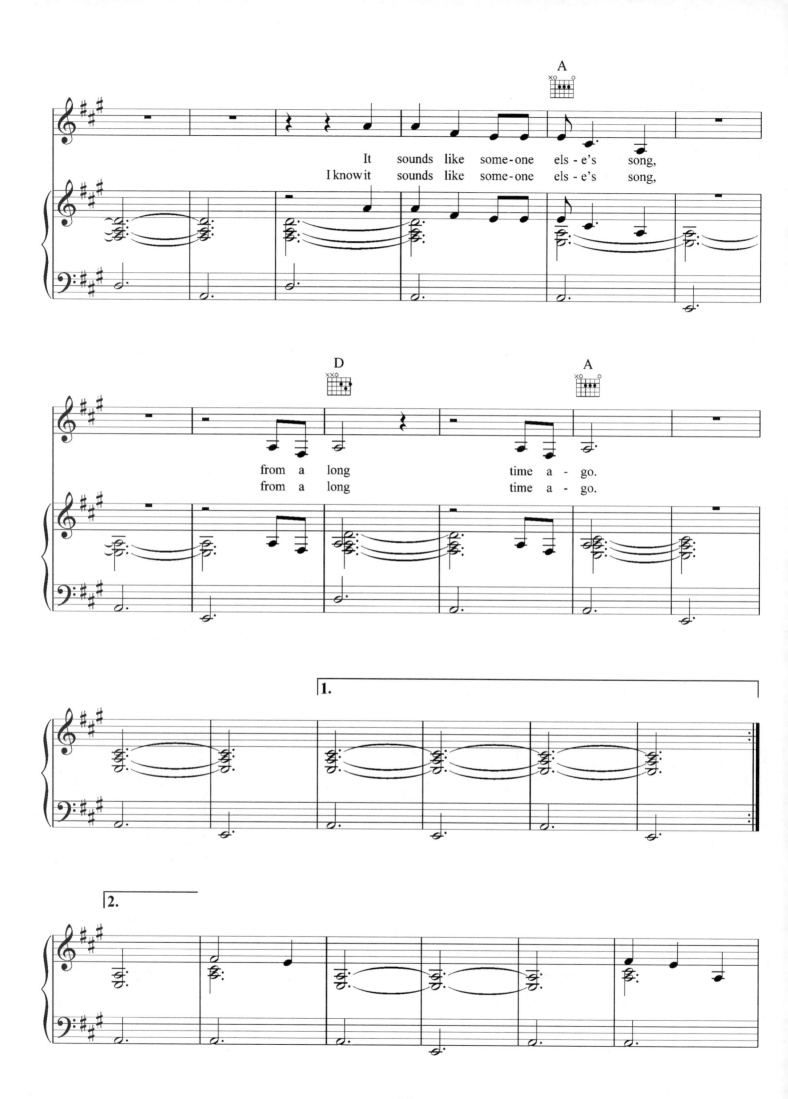

It sounds like some-one els-e's song,
I know it sounds like some-one els-e's song,

from a long time a-go.
from a long time a-go.

1.

2.

66

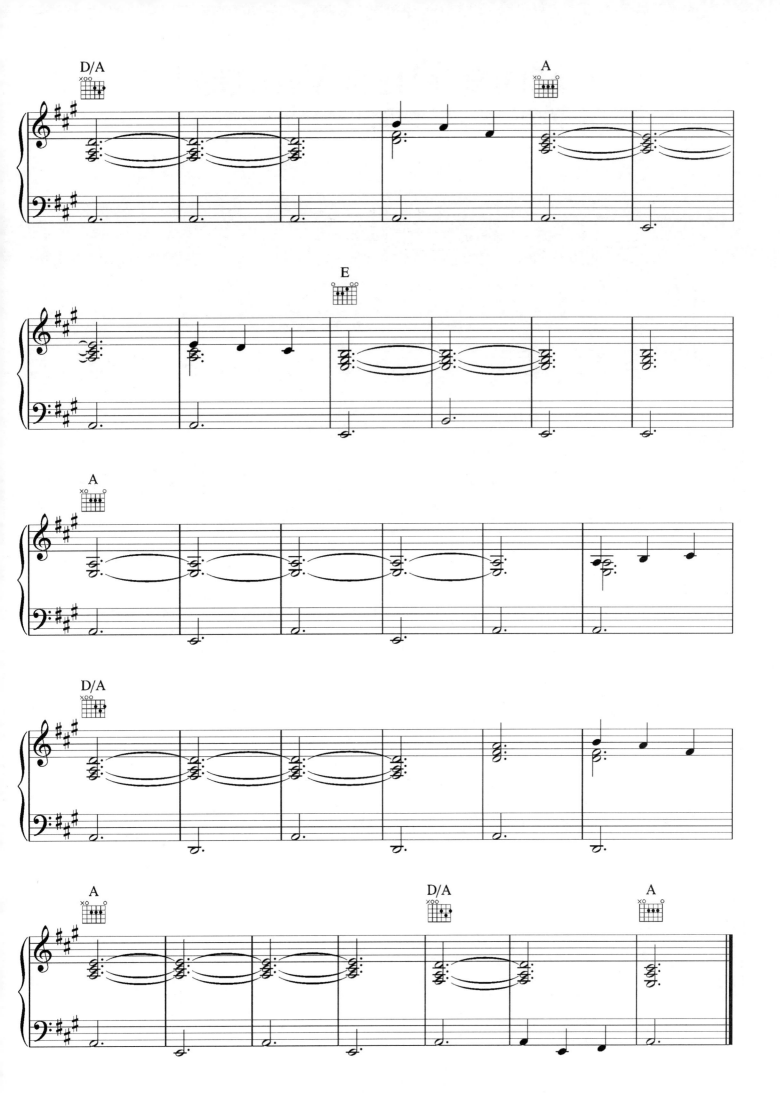

More Than Words

Words & Music by Nuno Bettencourt & Gary Cherone

1. Say - ing "I ___ love ___ you", is not the words I want ___
(Verse 2 see block lyric)

to ___ hear ___ from you, ___ it's not that I ___ want ___ you,

Verse 2:
Now I've tried to talk to you
And make you understand
All you have to do is close your eyes
And just reach out your hands
And touch me,
Hold me close don't ever let me go.
More than words
Is all I ever needed you to show
Then you wouldn't have to say
That you love me
'Cause I'd already know.

What would you do *etc.*

Over The Rainbow

Words by E.Y. Harburg
Music by Harold Arlen

and wake up where the clouds are far be-hind me.

Where trou-bles melt like le-mon drops a-way a-bove the chim-ney tops, that's where

Verse 2:
Somewhere over the rainbow
Skies are blue
And the dreams that you dared to dream
Really do come true.

I Don't Want To Talk About It

Words & Music by Danny Whitten

83

Otherwise

Words & Music by Paul Godfrey, Ross Godfrey & Skye Edwards

'cause you got to be seen_ to be play-ing the game.__
I wan-na take up your love_ but it's locked in a vault.__

Yes, we got to be seen_ to be play-ing the game.__
I wan-na take up your love_ but it's locked in a vault.__

It ain't gon-na hurt_ now, if you o-pen up your eyes._

You're mak-ing it worse_ now, ev-'ry time you crit-i-cise._

Sand And Water

Words & Music by Beth Nielsen Chapman

Original key F♯

I Want Your Love

Words & Music by Edwina Hayes

Hallelujah

Words & Music by Leonard Cohen

May-be there's a God a-bove, but all I've ev-er learned from love was how to shoot some-

Verse 3   Well, baby I've been here before
I've seen this room, and I've walked this floor,
You know, I used to live alone before I knew you
And I've seen your flag on the marble arch
And love is not a victory march
It's a cold and it's a broken Hallelujah

Verse 4   Well, there was a time when you let me know
What's really going on below
But now you never show that to me do ya?
But remember when I moved in you
And the holy dove was moving too
And every breath we drew was Hallelujah

Love Minus Zero

Words & Music by Bob Dylan

must hold___ a grudge.___

Sta-tutes made___ of match - sticks
(2° instrumental)

crum-ble in - to one an-oth-

- er.   My love winks, she does not bo - ther;___   she knows___

___ too much to ar - gue or to judge.

(1° tacet)
The___

Bad Day

Words & Music by Daniel Powter

Where is the mo - ment we need - ed the most?

You kick up the leaves, and the ma - gic is lost.

Cannonball

Words & Music by Damien Rice

There's still a lit-tle bit of your taste___ in my mouth. There's still a lit-tle bit of you laced___

There's still a lit-tle bit of your song___ in my ear. There's still a lit-tle bit of your words,___

___ I long to___ hear.___ You step a lit-tle clos-er to me,___

D.S. al Coda

so close that I___ can't see what's go-ing on.__

Coda

float like a can - non. Stones taught me to fly.__

Love taught me to cry.__ So come on, cou-rage, teach me to be shy,

'cause it's not hard__ to fall,__ and I don't wan-na scare__ her. It's not

Thank You

Words & Music by Dido Armstrong & Paul Herman

thank you for giv-ing me the best day of my life. And

oh, just to be with you is hav-ing the best day of my

life. *Pipe*

Wishing I Was There

Words & Music by Natalie Imbruglia, Colin Campsie & Phil Thornalley

Take your

Good People

Words & Music by Jack Johnson

this and that, with a rat-tle a tat, test-ing___ one, two, now what__ ya gon-na do? Bad

news, mis-used, got too much too lose. Gim-me some truth, now who's__ side are we on? What-

-ev-er you say, turn on the boob tube, I'm in the mood to o-bey. So

lead me a-stray, by the way___ now: Where'd all the good peo-ple

140

Sit - ting 'round, feel - ing far a - way.___

So far a - way___ but I can feel the de - bris. Can you feel___ it?

You in - ter - rupt me from a friend - ly con - ver - sa - tion,

to tell me how great___ it's all___ gon - na be.___

Nightswimming

Words & Music by Peter Buck, Michael Mills,
Michael Stipe & William Berry

147

The pho-to-graph__ re - flects,__ ev-'ry street__ light a__ re - mind - er. Night swim-ming de-

-serves a qui - et night,___ de-

-serves a qui - et night.___

Hey Sweet Man

Words & Music by Madeleine Peyroux

Hey___ mom-ma's child,   ain't you been wait - ing___ for me?

Got a mind   to love you.   my love___ won't leave you be.___

Hey sweet__ wo - man,__ I see you're search-ing too.

How Wonderful You Are

Words & Music by Gordon Haskell

Lay Lady Lay

Words & Music by Bob Dylan

Strange & Beautiful
(I'll Put A Spell On You)

Words & Music by Matthew Hales & Kim Oliver

I've been watch-ing your world from a - far, I've been try-ing to be where you are. And I've been se-cret-ly fall-ing a-

171

Unintended

Words & Music by Matthew Bellamy

To Coda

175

74-75

Words & Music by Mike Connell

Original Key G#m

Got no rea - son   for com-ing to me __ and the rain __   run-ning down. __   There's no rea - son.

The Weakness In Me

Words & Music by Joan Armatrading

(Something Inside) So Strong

Words & Music by Labi Siffre

1. The high-er you build your bar-ri-ers the tall-er I be-come.
(Verse 2 see block lyric)

The fur - ther you take my rights a - way
the fast - er I will run.
You can de - ny me,
you can de - cide to turn your face a - way.
No mat - ter 'cause there's
some - thin' in - side so strong.
I know that I can make it,

189

though you're do-ing me wrong, so wrong. You thought that my pride was gone,— oh no.—

There's some-thin' in-side so strong.— Oh,— some-thin' in-side so strong.

Bro-thers and sis-ters

when they in-sist we're just not good e-nough,— mm,—

There's some-thin' in - side so strong._____ Oh,_____ some-thin' in - side so_____

strong.

D.%. al Coda

Verse 2:
The more you refuse to hear my voice
The louder I will sing
You hide behind walls of Jericho
Your lies will come tumbling
Deny my place in time
You squander wealth that's mine
My light will shine so brightly it will blind you.

'Cause there's somethin' inside so strong *etc.*

Cat's In The Cradle

Words & Music by Harry Chapin & Sandy Chapin

1. My child ar-rived__ just the o-ther day, he
(*Verses 2-4: see block lyrics*)

came to the world in the us-u-al way.__ But there were planes to catch__ and bills to pay,

Verse 2:

My son turned ten just the other day
He said, "Thanks for the ball, Dad, come on let's play
Can you teach me to throw?"
I said, "Not today, I got a lot to do"
He said, "That's OK"
And then, he walked away but a smile never came
He said, "I'm gonna be like him, yeah,
You know I'm gonna be like him."

Chorus

Verse 3:

Well, he came from college just the other day
So much like a man I had to say
"Son, I'm proud of you, can you sit for a while?"
He shook his head and he said with a smile
"What I'd really like, Dad, is to borrow the car keys
See you later, can I have them please?"

Chorus

Verse 4:

I've long since retired, my son's moved away
I called him up just the other day
I said, "I'd like to see you, if you don't mind"
He said, "I'd love to Dad, if I can find the time
You see my new job's a hassle and the kids have the flu
But it's sure nice talking to you, Dad
It's been sure nice talking to you"
And as I hung up the phone it occurred to me
He'd grown up just like me
My boy was just like me.

Chorus

Song To The Siren

Words & Music by Tim Buckley & Larry Beckett

Sky Blue And Black

Words & Music by Jackson Browne

1. In the call-ing out__ to one an-oth-er of the   lo - vers up and down the strand.__
2. Where the touch of the lov-er end and   the soul of the friend__ be-gins,__

You're the hid-den cost_ in the thing that's lost___ in ev-'ry-thing I do. Yeah,_____

___ and I'll ne-ver stop look-ing___ for you.__

In the sun-light and the sha-dows_ and the fa-ces of on the a - ven-ue.__

That's the way_ love is,__ that's the way_ love is,__

You Were Meant For Me

Words & Music by Jewel Kilcher & Steve Poltz

Original Key B major

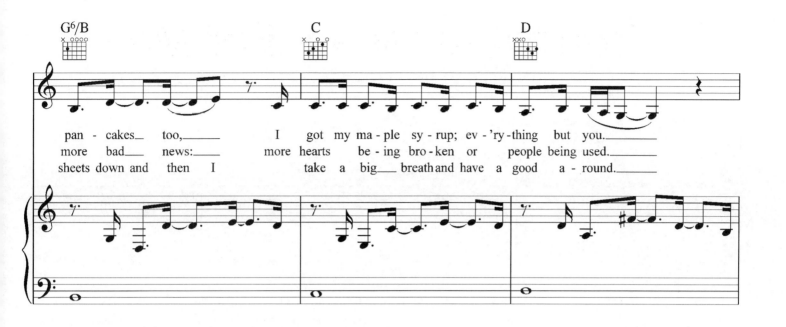

ne-ver put wet to-wels on the floor a-ny-more.___
it made me miss you,___ oh___ so bad 'cause:
just___should-n't think an-y-more_ to-night 'cause:

Dreams last___ so___ long,___

e - ven af-ter you're gone.___ I know that you loved_ me_ and

soon you___will see___ you were meant for me,___ and I___ was meant for

you.

I go a-bout my bus-'ness, I'm

To Coda ⊕

Perfect Day

Words & Music by Lou Reed

then la - ter a mo - vie too and then home. Oh

it's such a per - fect day— I'm glad I spent it with you

oh such a per - fect day,— you just keep me hang - ing on,— you just

1.
keep me hang - ing on.

2.
keep me hang - ing on.

Verse 2:
Just a perfect day
Problems all left alone
Weekenders on our own,
It's such fun.
Just a perfect day
You made me forget myself
I thought I was someone else,
Someone good.

2/07 (61450) 23456789